T0197566

Berry Boy

In the Buffalo Days

WRITTEN BY **Kathleen A. Connelly Kipp**

ILLUSTRATED BY **Moriah Ann Kipp**

To order additional copies of this book, contact:
Xlibris
844-714-8691
www.Xlibris.com
Orders@Xlibris.com

ISBN: Softcover   978-1-4535-1703-1
        Hardcover   978-1-4535-1704-8
        EBook   978-1-6698-1689-8

Print information available on the last page

Rev. date: 03/17/2022

Introduction

This book is set in the early 1800's during the time of the horse culture. Blackfeet Indians acquired the horse in the 1600-1700's. It was a time of minimal European contact and before the westward expansion reached the Blackfeet. It is based on historical hunting practices of the Blackfeet Indians or Pikuni (Small Scabby Robes) as they were known to other Tribes. The Blackfeet called themselves Nitsitapi (Neetseetahpee) or Real People. They followed the Buffalo as a way of life for thousands of years from the Yellowstone River in Southern Montana to the Saskatchewan River in the north, the Headwaters of the Missouri River to the east and in the Rocky Mountains to the west. Lewis and Clark did not discover Montana. The Blackfeet were there, thriving in their environment.

The Blackfeet loved their children more than anything. The taking of land and loss of buffalo, starvation, and European diseases destroyed the Blackfeet's ability to be self-sufficient. The final straw was the killing of over 200 children, women, and a few elderly men, including Chief Heavy Runner, at the Bear River (Marias River) on a freezing cold morning of January 23, 1870.

The Blackfeet survivors were heartbroken and forced to give up their remaining children to institutionalized abuse called Boarding Schools in the United States and Residential Schools in Canada. The Blackfeet language and culture was forbidden.

After the elimination of the great buffalo herds by the railroad; the Blackfeet were forced to stay on small pieces of land called reservations. The Blackfeet's territorial hunting-gathering land base was decreased by a series of executive orders and treaties. It started with the Fort Laramie Treaty of 1851, where the Blackfeet were not present. A few years later came the Lame Bull Treaty of 1855. Next were executive orders by President Grant in 1873 – 1874. The Blackfeet Territory originally consisted of most of Montana and into Alberta and Saskatchewan, Canada.

Today, the Blackfeet Reservation boundary is north on the Canadian border, south on Birch Creek, east on Cut Bank Creek, and west is Glacier National Park for one and a half million acres in north central Montana.

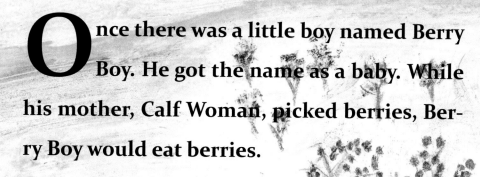

O nce there was a little boy named Berry Boy. He got the name as a baby. While his mother, Calf Woman, picked berries, Berry Boy would eat berries.

Fresh berries were his favorite. He also loved roasted buffalo meat.

As Berry Boy grew older, he spent more time at school. His school was somewhat different than school now, but yet with the same goal. When he went to school he was being taught what he would need to know as an adult.

Now at seven years of age, Berry Boy was learning many skills. The old men were the teachers. They showed the boys how to make arrows, bows, arrowheads, traps, and how to use them. The young boys were also becoming good at riding horses (punokomitah).

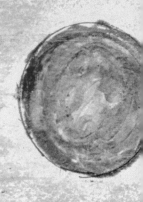

Berry Boy liked to ride horses and he would dream about going out on his first buffalo (enee) hunt. He would practice guiding his horse by using his legs and shifting his weight. A good buffalo hunter would need to have a well trained horse so that his hands would be free to handle his bow and arrow.

One day his father, who was called the Heavy Runner because he was very good at running for long distances said,

"Berry Boy, I see that you have been training hard. You may ride along on the next hunt."

The day of the buffalo hunt had come. The women and girls tied leather packs to the travois. The hunter put a braided hair bridle and leather cinch with a hide pad onto their horses.

The approach to the grazing buffalo was important. Using coulees and buttes to keep out of sight helped the hunters get close. They also had to travel into the wind so that the buffalo would not smell their scent.

This was the moon, when chokecherries ripen, or August. The hunters would be trying to get bulls. Cows are thin from nursing their calves during this moon.

Once the hunters were near a herd of buffalo, they would race their horses close. The chase began as the hunters picked out an animal to shoot. They would aim for the rib area on the buffalo.

Berry Boy rode hard and fast. The buffalo herd shook the earth as their hooves pounded the ground. There was plenty of buffalo. Even Berry Boy brought down a buffalo calf.

Everyone was thankful for a successful hunt when the butchering started. The women and girls cut meat from the bone and sliced pieces thinly. They hung the meat pieces onto drying racks with a small fire below.

After the meat was cut and dried, Calf Woman and the other females of the tribe would work on the buffalo hides. They stretched and scraped the hides with bone scrapers.

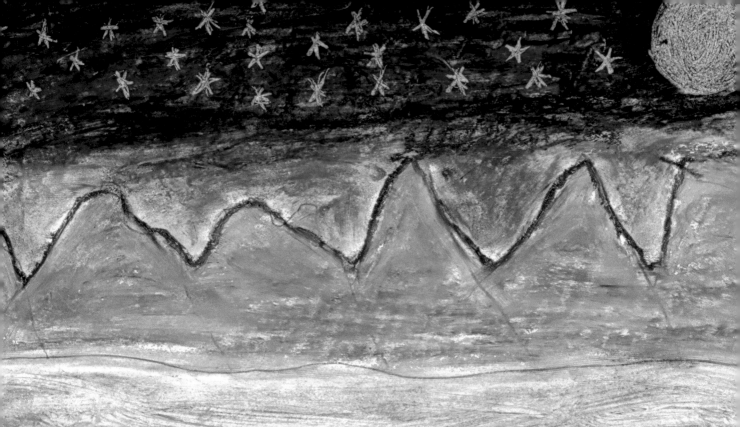

The buffalo parts were used to make over eighty different items. Horns were used to make spoons and cups. Buffalo hides provided the Blackfeet with moccasins, blankets, and teepees. A buffalo hide blanket was very warm and would keep Berry Boy warm when the temperature would dip down to forty degrees below zero in the winter time. Berry boy braided the buffalo hair into strong rope.

Berry Boy and the Blackfeet people were content. They kept busy making both practical and decorative items. In the evenings they would tell and retell stories. The young Blackfeet enjoyed listening about the past. Now Berry Boy has a story to tell.

Glossary

Blackfeet Vocabulary

Punokahmitah – horse

Enee – buffalo

Punokah – elk

Imitah - dog

Printed in the United States
by Baker & Taylor Publisher Services